Team Spirit

THE MINNESOTA TIMBERWOLVES

BY

MARK STEWART

Content Consultant
Matt Zeysing
Historian and Archivist
The Naismith Memorial Basketball Hall of Fame

NORWOOD HOUSE PRESS

CHICAGO, ILLINOIS

Norwood House Press
P.O. Box 316598
Chicago, Illinois 60631

For information regarding Norwood House Press, please visit our website at:
www.norwoodhousepress.com or call 866-565-2900.

All photos courtesy of Getty Images except the following:
General Mills, Inc. (6), Topps, Inc. (14, 20, 34 left, 35 top left, 38, 43),
Sports Illustrated/Time Inc. (16), Black Book Partners Archive (36).
Cover Photo: Noah Graham/Getty Images
Special thanks to Topps, Inc.

Editor: Mike Kennedy
Designer: Ron Jaffe
Project Management: Black Book Partners, LLC.

Special thanks to Wendy Woodfill and Barbara McMillan

Library of Congress Cataloging-in-Publication Data

Stewart, Mark, 1960-
   The Minnesota Timberwolves / by Mark Stewart ; content consultant, Matt
Zeysing.
      p. cm. -- (Team spirit)
   Includes bibliographical references and index.
   Summary: "Presents the history and accomplishments of the Minnesota
Timberwolves basketball team. Includes highlights of players, coaches, and
awards, quotes, timelines, maps, glossary, and websites"--Provided by
publisher.
   ISBN-13: 978-1-59953-291-2 (library edition : alk. paper)
   ISBN-10: 1-59953-291-3 (library edition : alk. paper) 1. Minnesota
Timberwolves (Basketball team)--History--Juvenile literature. I. Zeysing,
Matt. II. Title.
   GV885.52.M565S74 2009
   796.323'64097795759--dc22

                                                          2008044961

COVER PHOTO: The Timberwolves celebrate a win during the 2007–08 season.

Table of Contents

SPORTS WORDS & VOCABULARY WORDS: In this book, you will find many words that are new to you. You may also see familiar words used in new ways. The glossary on page 46 gives the meanings of basketball words, as well as "everyday" words that have special basketball meanings. These words appear in **bold type** throughout the book. The glossary on page 47 gives the meanings of vocabulary words that are not related to basketball. They appear in ***bold italic type*** throughout the book.

BASKETBALL SEASONS: Because each basketball season begins late in one year and ends early in the next, seasons are not named after years. Instead, they are written out as two years separated by a dash, for example 1944–45 or 2005–06.

Meet the Timberwolves

Timberwolves hunt in a pack. Every member has an important job to do. They follow strong leaders and track their prey until the moment is right. Then they strike. This is how the Minnesota Timberwolves play. They are fast and fearless—and always ready to pounce.

Like a pack of timberwolves, the team has had amazing leaders and excellent **role players**. They move quickly and strike hard. Sometimes the "T-Wolves" win and sometimes they lose, but they never let up. Once they get a taste of victory, they don't let go.

This book tells the story of the Timberwolves. Their playing style makes them a fun team to watch, but they are not fun to play. That is why the fans in Minnesota love their team. They have always rooted hard for players who give their all. In fact, when they watch the T-Wolves in action, they sometimes see a little bit of themselves.

Kevin Love, Al Jefferson, and Mike Miller pose for a picture before the 2008–09 season.

Way Back When

Long before the Timberwolves played their first **National Basketball Association (NBA)** game, Minneapolis was a city of champions. From 1948 to 1960, the Lakers played there. During that time, they won five NBA championships. Their stars included George Mikan, Jim Pollard, and Slater Martin. In the late 1960s, Minneapolis was also home to two teams in the **American Basketball Association (ABA)**. Among the stars on those clubs were Mel Daniels and Connie Hawkins.

GEORGE MIKAN
CENTER, MINNEAPOLIS LAKERS

During the 1980s, the city pushed to get another team. Mikan helped convince the NBA to return to Minneapolis. The Timberwolves took the court for the 1989–90 season. They built their team with **draft picks** and unwanted players from other NBA clubs. Tony Campbell, Tyrone Corbin, Pooh Richardson, and Sam Mitchell led Minnesota into battle that first year. The Timberwolves played excellent defense but finished with only 22 victories.

Minnesota added several talented players over the next few years, including Christian Laettner and Isaiah Rider. However, the team could not improve in the **standings**. That began to change in 1995, when the Timberwolves brought in Kevin McHale to run the team. McHale had won three championships as a member of the Boston Celtics. He knew how to build a winner.

McHale started by drafting Kevin Garnett, a high school player who jumped straight into the NBA. Garnett played every minute as if it were his last. His *enthusiasm* rubbed off on his teammates. McHale also made trades for forward Tom Gugliotta and guard Stephon Marbury. These three young players were among the most exciting stars in the NBA. In 1996–97, they led the T-Wolves to the **playoffs** for the first time.

The Timberwolves had their first 50-win season in 1999–00. Garnett now teamed with Terrell Brandon, Wally Szczerbiak, Malik Sealy, and Joe Smith. Minnesota looked like a club on the rise. Unfortunately, the T-Wolves suffered several *setbacks*. The worst came when Sealy was killed in a car accident. The team struggled to recover from this tragedy. Later, Smith left Minnesota after a problem with his contract.

LEFT: George Mikan, the leader of the Minneapolis Lakers.
ABOVE: Tom Gugliotta drives to the basket.

Despite these setbacks, Garnett continued to improve, and the Timberwolves always found a way to make the **postseason**. The problem was that they could not win in the first round. Minnesota lost its opening series seven years in a row!

Finally, in 2003–04, the Timberwolves advanced deep into the playoffs. That season, Garnett was named the league's **Most Valuable Player (MVP)**. He led a talented roster that included Sam Cassell and Latrell Sprewell. Both had played in the **NBA Finals** before. The T-Wolves won 58 games and finished as **Midwest Division** champions for the first time. They beat the Denver Nuggets and Sacramento Kings in the playoffs to reach the **Western Conference Finals**.

Minnesota's luck ran out against the Los Angeles Lakers. An injury to Cassell left the team without an *experienced* point guard. The Timberwolves put up a great fight, but Minnesota lost in six games. They had come within two victories of the NBA Finals.

Some felt that the aging T-Wolves could not go any further. In 2004, Minnesota started to think about rebuilding again. No one doubted that this had to be done. There was one question—would the team do it while Garnett was still a superstar?

LEFT: Kevin Garnett rises for a jump shot. He was Minnesota's best player for more than 10 years.   **ABOVE**: Latrell Sprewell and Sam Cassell

The Team Today

In 2007, the Timberwolves had to make a difficult decision. Kevin Garnett deserved to play for a championship **contender**. He had given everything he had to the T-Wolves, but it simply wasn't enough. Minnesota did not have enough good players to reach the NBA Finals before Garnett retired. The Timberwolves began to look for a trade that would help their star achieve his dream—and also give Minnesota fans a brighter future.

The Timberwolves found a perfect fit with Kevin McHale's old team, the Boston Celtics. Garnett was traded for five players—including young stars Al Jefferson and Ryan Gomes—and two draft choices. One year later, Garnett had his championship ring, and the Timberwolves had an exciting, young club again.

Jefferson and Gomes teamed up with Randy Foye, Mike Miller, Rashad McCants, and Kevin Love. This collection of young stars gave the Timberwolves many of the pieces they would need to complete the championship puzzle. As these players grew together, the team prepared for another run at the NBA Finals.

Ryan Gomes offers words of advice to Rashad McCants during the 2007–08 season.

Home Court

The Timberwolves' first home was the Hubert H. Humphrey Metrodome. The stadium was actually built for the Twins baseball team and the Vikings football team. It was not ideal for basketball, but the T-Wolves didn't mind it. The team was able to sell a lot of tickets because they had so many extra seats to fill.

In 1990, the T-Wolves moved into a new arena in downtown Minneapolis. They share it with the Lynx of the **Women's National Basketball Association (WNBA)**. The arena often hosts high school basketball tournaments, too. In 2004, it was *modernized* with new seats and an LED scoreboard. The team also made improvements that enabled more wheelchair-bound fans to attend games.

Minnesota used to be one of only three teams to use a *unique* surface known as a parquet floor. The team switched to a regular hardwood court before the 2008–09 season.

BY THE NUMBERS

- *The Timberwolves' arena has 20,500 seats for basketball.*
- *The arena cost $104 million to build in 1990.*
- *As of 2008, the Timberwolves have retired only one number—2, which belonged to Malik Sealy.*

The Timberwolves host a game in their arena during the 2006–07 season.

Dressed for Success

When the NBA announced that it had awarded Minnesota a new team, no one could agree on a good name. Fans submitted more than 1,200 different ideas in a contest. The choices were narrowed down to *Timberwolves* and *Polars*. The team put it to a vote among all the city councils in Minnesota. It made sense that *Timberwolves* won out. There are more timberwolves in Minnesota than in any state other than Alaska.

The team's main colors were blue and green in 1989–90. The **logo** showed a proud-looking wolf. The trim on the uniform used tiny pine trees to form a cool zig-zag design. In 1996, black was added to

the uniforms, and a new logo was created. It showed a snarling wolf behind a line of pine trees. In 2008, the team **unveiled** another new uniform and logo. The uniform tops used the name *Wolves*. The logo featured a basketball with a howling wolf inside of it.

Christian Laettner models the uniform from the team's early years.

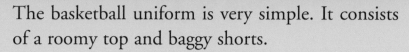

The basketball uniform is very simple. It consists of a roomy top and baggy shorts.

- The top hangs from the shoulders, with big "scoops" for the arms and neck. This style has not changed much over the years.

- Shorts, however, have changed a lot. They used to be very short, so players could move their legs freely. In the last 20 years, shorts have actually gotten longer and much baggier.

Basketball uniforms look the same as they did long ago … until you look very closely. In the old days, the shorts had belts and buckles. The tops were made of a thick cotton called "jersey," which got very heavy when players sweated. Later, uniforms were made of shiny **satin**. They may have looked great, but they did not "breathe." Players got very hot! Today, most uniforms are made of **synthetic** materials that soak up sweat and keep the body cool.

Randy Foye wears the team's 2008–09 home uniform.

We Won!

When Minnesota basketball fans get together to relive the Timberwolves' greatest moments, talk always turns to the 2004 playoffs. That spring the team won its opening-round series for the first time ever. The T-Wolves beat Carmelo Anthony and the

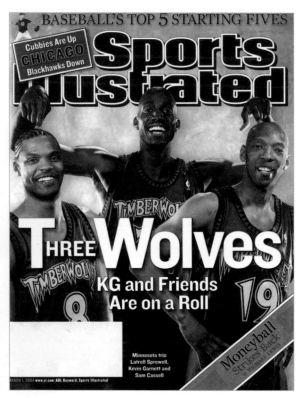

Denver Nuggets in five games.

Their next opponent was the Sacramento Kings. They gave the Timberwolves the fight of their lives. In Game 1, Sam Cassell and Sacramento's Mike Bibby went head-to-head in a thrilling shootout. Cassell outscored Bibby 40 to 33, but the Kings won the game, 104–98. Minnesota was in danger of losing Game 2, but Cassell led a great *comeback*. He scored eight points in the final minutes, and the T-Wolves earned a 94–89 victory.

Game 3 was another great battle. A few days before the contest, the T-Wolves learned that Kevin Garnett had been named NBA MVP. He celebrated by scoring 30 points, including the game-winning shot with

10 seconds left in **overtime**. In Game 4, the two teams fought over every rebound and loose ball. The Kings won 87–81 and tied the series.

Game 5 was another defensive struggle. Latrell Sprewell was the only player on either team to find his rhythm. The Timberwolves had added the energetic and emotional Sprewell to their club for games like these. He sliced through the Sacramento defense for 34 points, and the T-Wolves won 86–74. Sprewell played well again in Game 6, but it was not enough to stop the Kings on their home court. They tied the series with a 104–87 win.

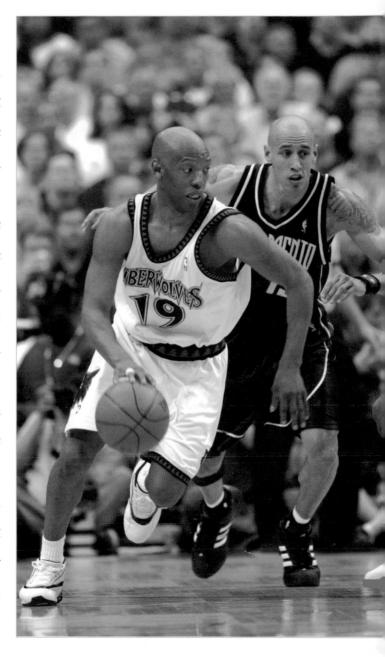

LEFT: As this issue of *Sports Illustrated* shows, Latrell Sprewell, Kevin Garnett, and Sam Cassell made the Timberwolves front-page news in 2004.
ABOVE: Cassell, the hero of Game 2 against the Sacramento Kings.

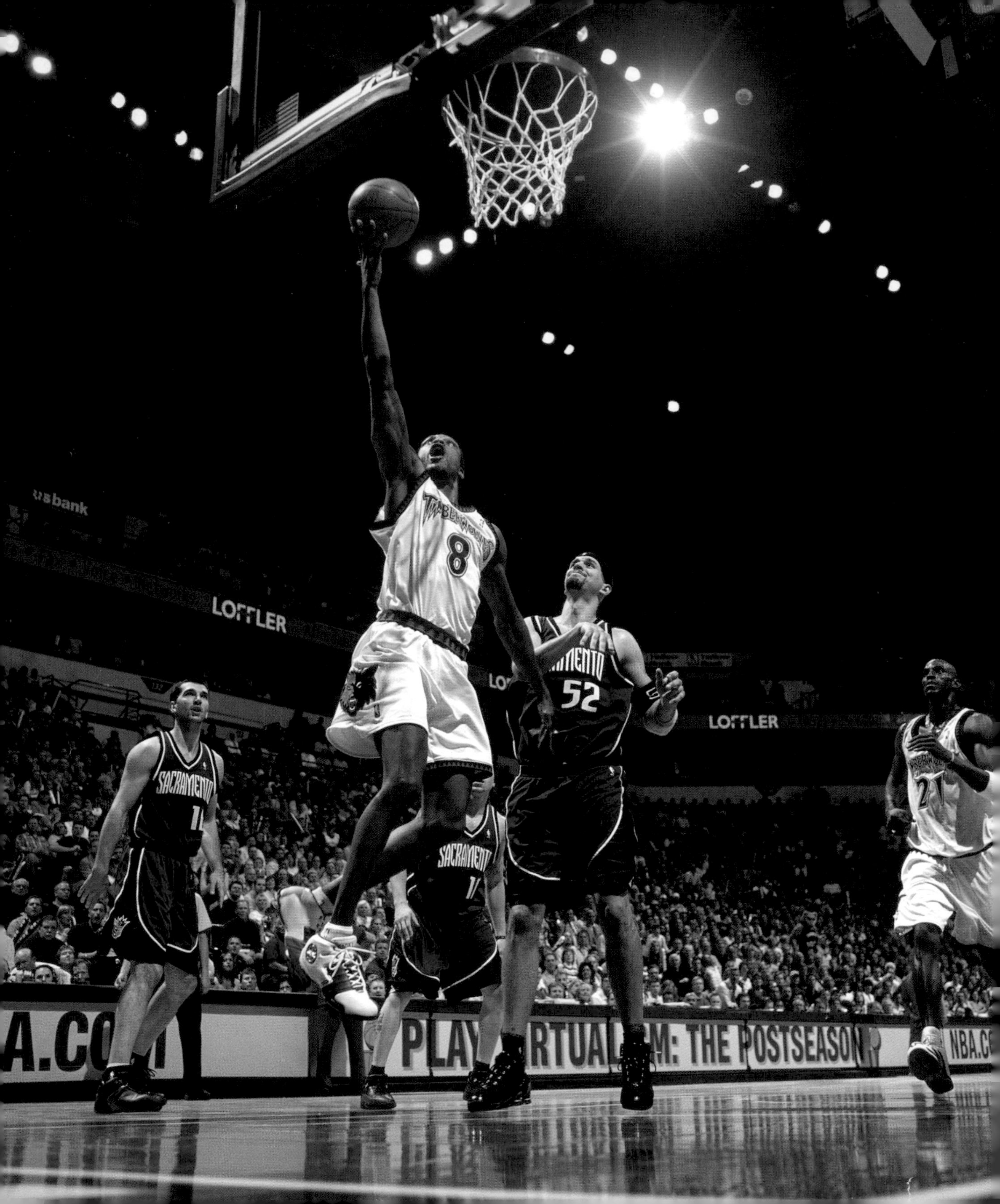

8
52
SACRAMENTO

During the game, Anthony Peeler of the Kings hit Garnett in the face with an elbow. Garnett kept his cool, and then used the incident to get fired up for Game 7. He scored 32 points and grabbed 21 rebounds in a game that was close until the final buzzer.

The T-Wolves led 83–80 when Doug Christie launched a long **3-pointer** for Sacramento. His shot missed everything, but Brad Miller retrieved the ball

and tried to make a layup. Garnett swatted the ball into the seats. Sacramento next got the ball to Chris Webber, who had a good look at the basket. He launched a 3-point shot as time ran out. The ball rolled around the rim and then out.

Webber fell to his knees. Garnett leaped onto the scorer's table in glee and soaked up the cheers of the crowd in the Target Center. Earlier in the day, Garnett had celebrated his 28th birthday. "I've had some real special presents on my birthday, but nothing like this!" he shouted.

LEFT: Latrell Sprewell converts a layup against the Kings.
ABOVE: Garnett shoots over Chris Webber in Game 7.

Go-To Guys

To be a true star in the NBA, you need more than a great shot. You have to be a "go-to guy"—someone teammates trust to make the winning play when the seconds are ticking away in a big game. Timberwolves fans have had a lot to cheer about over the years, including these great stars …

THE PIONEERS

TONY CAMPBELL   6′ 7″ Forward

• BORN: 5/7/1962   • PLAYED FOR TEAM: 1989–90 TO 1991–92

Tony Campbell was a great shooter who spent five years sitting on the bench with two other teams. In his first year with the Timberwolves, he set a team record by averaging 23.2 points per game.

POOH RICHARDSON   6′ 1″ Guard

• BORN: 5/14/1966

• PLAYED FOR TEAM: 1989–90 TO 1991–92

Jerome "Pooh" Richardson was Minnesota's point guard during the team's early years. He was a good **playmaker** and defender. Richardson led the team in **assists** three years in a row.

ABOVE: Pooh Richardson   **RIGHT**: Doug West

SAM MITCHELL   6´ 7˝ Forward

- BORN: 9/2/1963
- PLAYED FOR TEAM: 1989–90 TO 1991–92 & 1995–96 TO 2001–02

Sam Mitchell was a good scorer and rebounder. He was also a good leader. When Kevin Garnett joined the T-Wolves as a teenager, Mitchell helped him learn the ins and outs of life in the NBA.

DOUG WEST   6´ 6˝ Guard

- BORN: 5/27/1967
- PLAYED FOR TEAM: 1989–90 TO 1997–98

During his time in Minnesota, Doug West was one of the team's most reliable players. Whether starting or coming off the bench, he gave the Timberwolves whatever they needed. West was the team's top scorer in 1992–93.

CHRISTIAN LAETTNER   6´ 11˝ Center

- BORN: 8/17/1969
- PLAYED FOR TEAM: 1992–93 TO 1995–96

Christian Laettner was used to winning in college. So joining a young team like the Timberwolves was a shock. But that didn't stop Laettner from doing it all for Minnesota. He was named to the NBA's **All-Rookie** team in 1992–93.

KEVIN GARNETT   6´ 11˝ Forward/Center

- BORN: 5/19/1976
- PLAYED FOR TEAM: 1995–96 TO 2006–07

For a dozen incredible seasons, Kevin Garnett was the heart and soul of the Timberwolves. He was fierce on defense and brilliant with the ball in his hands. "KG" was a member of the **All-NBA** team eight times with the T-Wolves.

TERRELL BRANDON   5´ 11˝ Guard

- BORN: 5/20/1970
- PLAYED FOR TEAM: 1998–99 TO 2001–02

Terrell Brandon was a good player on the court and a great contributor in the community. Few NBA players have ever been closer to their fans. Brandon was injured for much of his time in Minnesota. When he was healthy, he was one of the league's best guards.

WALLY SZCZERBIAK   6´ 7˝ Forward

- BORN: 3/5/1977   • PLAYED FOR TEAM: 1999–00 TO 2005–06

Wally Szczerbiak grew up in Spain, where his father was a **professional** basketball star. He learned every trick in the book when it came to shooting and scoring. Szczerbiak once scored 44 points in a game for the T-Wolves.

ABOVE: Kevin Garnett   **RIGHT**: Al Jefferson

SAM CASSELL   6´ 3˝ Guard

• BORN: 11/18/1969   • PLAYED FOR TEAM: 2003–04 TO 2004–05

Sam Cassell played for only two years in Minnesota, but the fans never forgot him. In his first season with the Timberwolves, he averaged 19.8 points a game and led the team to the Western Conference Finals.

AL JEFFERSON   6´ 10˝ Forward

• BORN: 1/4/1985

• FIRST SEASON WITH TEAM: 2007–08

When the T-Wolves traded for Al Jefferson, they got a player who reminded many fans of a young Kevin Garnett. Jefferson was quick, strong, and *aggressive* when he had the ball near the basket. Before long, he became a team leader.

KEVIN LOVE   6´ 10˝ Forward/Center

• BORN: 9/7/1988

• FIRST SEASON WITH TEAM: 2008–09

No matter what position he played, Kevin Love made things tough for Minnesota's opponents during his **rookie** year. He came to the NBA with the shooting and passing skills of a guard. But he put those skills to use in the body of a center.

On the Sidelines

Coaching the Timberwolves has been one of the toughest jobs in the NBA. Minnesota fans know their basketball, and they are also very passionate about their team. If a coach makes a poor decision, he hears about it on the court, on the radio, and probably at home, too! Among the men who have accepted this challenge are Bill Musselman, Sidney Lowe, Dwane Casey, and Randy Wittman.

Minnesota's most successful coach was Flip Saunders. He was hired by Kevin McHale. The two had been college teammates at the University of Minnesota. They continued their partnership with the Timberwolves.

Saunders took over as coach in 1995–96. He won more than 400 games during his career and led the team to the Western Conference Finals once. He placed great trust in team leaders and was *patient* with young players as they worked their way into the lineup. Saunders demanded only one thing from the Timberwolves—a full effort on defense every game.

This picture shows (from left to right) Randy Wittman, Flip Saunders, Jerry Sichting, and Sidney Lowe. At the time, Saunders was the team's head coach, and Wittman, Lowe, and Sichting were his assistants.

One Great Day

The 2003 NBA **All-Star Game** was supposed to be Michael Jordan's "farewell" to the league and its fans. Kevin Garnett had other plans. He made the contest his own.

In a close and exciting game, Jordan made a shot to give the East a one-point lead with under five seconds to play in overtime. Kobe Bryant then tied the score with a free throw for the West. That sent the game into a second overtime.

From then on, it was all "KG." At one point, he matched up against Vince Carter of the East. Three times in a row, he used his size and quickness to hit short jump shots over Carter. Fans were amazed. Garnett was a forward! But when coach Phil Jackson asked him to play guard, he didn't hesitate.

26

LEFT: Kevin Garnett soars for a monster dunk during the 2003 All-Star Game.
RIGHT: Garnett gives a warm hug to Michael Jordan.

Garnett added a free throw to give his team a seven-point lead early in the second overtime. The West held on to win 155–145. Garnett finished with 37 points, nine rebounds, and five steals. He was named the game's MVP. The last player to score that many points in an All-Star Game was Jordan, who had 40 in 1988.

Like everyone else in Atlanta that night, Garnett thought Jordan would take home the MVP award after he made his shot in overtime. "It looked like old twenty-three crept back in the building and was trying to take the game," Garnett remembers. "But for the most part, we hung together and won. The All-Star Game is not about individuals. It's totally a group effort. It's a time for you to share stories, good times, emotional times with your teammates."

"I wanted it to be a competitive game," Jordan recalls. "It was a fun ending any way you look at it."

Legend Has It

Which Minnesota player invented the East Bay Funk Dunk?

LEGEND HAS IT that Isaiah Rider did. Rider was a rookie with the Timberwolves when he took the court in the 1994 NBA Slam Dunk Contest. Rider made several powerful dunks to reach the finals. When he threw an alley-oop pass to himself and slammed it through the hoop, fans thought they had seen his best dunk. They were wrong! Rider (who is from Oakland, in the East Bay region of California) started the "East Bay Funk Dunk" in the left corner. He dribbled down the **baseline**, rose into the air, passed the ball between his legs—and jammed as he flew past the rim. Picking the contest winner was a no-brainer after that.

ABOVE: Isaiah Rider holds up his Slam Dunk trophy.
RIGHT: Christian Laettner

Which member of the Timberwolves tried to buy a basketball and baseball team?

LEGEND HAS IT that Christian Laettner did. After his playing days, Laettner tried to buy the Memphis Grizzlies. He and his partners could not raise enough money, so he was not able to make the purchase. Before this, Laettner bought a share of the Phoenix Firebirds, a minor-league baseball team. Later he bought a share of the D.C. United soccer club.

Did the Timberwolves almost move to New Orleans?

LEGEND HAS IT that they did. In 1994, team owners Marv Wolfenson and Harvey Ratner put the T-Wolves up for sale. A group from Louisiana tried to buy the team. The NBA had a different idea. The league wanted the club to stay in Minnesota, partly because the state had some of the most loyal fans in the NBA. Glen Taylor knew this, too. With the support of the NBA, he bought the T-Wolves and kept them in Minneapolis.

It Really Happened

Unforgettable shots aren't always planned. Sometimes they just happen. During a game against the Sacramento Kings in the 1994–95 season, the Timberwolves ran the ball up the court. Isaiah Rider positioned himself along the left sideline and signaled for the ball. Rider was getting ready to drive to the basket, but the pass was behind him.

Rider tried to change direction and catch the pass but lost his balance. Both he and the ball began to head out of bounds. Rider caught the ball in his right hand while he jumped over the sideline. Everyone expected him to toss the ball toward midcourt. Rider, however, did not want to throw a pass to one of the Kings for an easy layup.

Instead, Rider flung the ball over his left shoulder, high in the air, with his back to the basket. Christian Laettner thought for a moment that his teammate was passing to him. But he watched with everyone else as the ball sailed over his head. All he could do was smile when Rider's "save" hit nothing but net for a 3-point play!

Tom Hanneman, the team's TV announcer, called Rider's shot the "play of the decade." Toward the end of the season, Rider won an *ESPY Award* for the best NBA play of the year.

Isaiah Rider eyes the rim during the 1994 Slam Dunk Contest. He was no stranger to incredible shots.

Team Spirit

The Timberwolves have tested the patience of their fans at times, but the fans always support them. In 1989–90, the team set an NBA record by selling more than a million tickets to their 41 home games. Since that season, millions more people have watched the T-Wolves play.

The Timberwolves have repaid the city's loyalty by sending players into the community to connect with young people. The team stresses reading skills and academic achievement. Every year, the T-Wolves offer college scholarships to top students. The players also donate jerseys and autographed basketballs and appear at charity events across the state to help raise money for good causes.

Inside the arena, the Timberwolves connect with their fans through contests, special theme nights, and different kinds of entertainment. The Timberwolves Dancers perform throughout the game. So does Crunch, the team's rim-rocking, motorcycle-riding *mascot*. Crunch can be seen all over Minnesota throughout the year.

Crunch entertains the Minnesota fans with fantastic dunks.

Timeline

The basketball season is played from October through June. That means each season takes place at the end of one year and the beginning of the next. In this timeline, the accomplishments of the Timberwolves are shown by season.

1993–94
The All-Star Game is played in the T-Wolves' arena.

1997–98
The Timberwolves win their first playoff game.

1989–90
The Timberwolves play their first season.

1995–96
The team drafts high school star Kevin Garnett.

1996–97
The T-Wolves reach the playoffs for the first time.

Kevin Garnett

Stephon Marbury, a star for the team in the late 1990s.

Wally
Szczerbiak

Kevin
McHale

1999–00
Wally Szczerbiak makes the
NBA All-Rookie team.

2004–05
Kevin McHale coaches
the team for 31 games.

2001–02
The Timberwolves beat the
Chicago Bulls by 53 points.

2003–04
Sam Cassell and Latrell
Sprewell join the team.

2007–08
The T-Wolves trade Kevin
Garnett for seven players.

Sam Cassell and
Latrell Sprewell

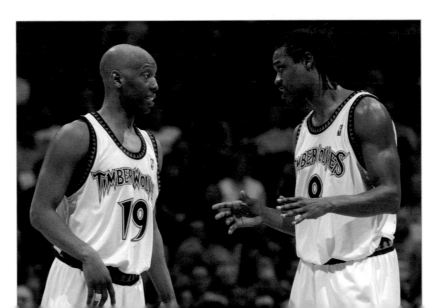

Fun Facts

SPECIAL K

In 2002–03, Kevin Garnett became only the third player in NBA history to lead his team in points, rebounds, assists, steals, and blocked shots. The first two were Dave Cowens of the Boston Celtics and Scottie Pippen of the Chicago Bulls.

HALL OF FAME GAME

Kevin Love's middle name is Wesley. He was named after Wes Unseld, who is a member of the **Basketball Hall of Fame**. Unseld was a friend and teammate of Kevin's dad, Stan. Kevin chose to wear number 42 to honor another Hall of Famer, Connie Hawkins.

LONG SHOT

In 2007–08, backup guard Rashad McCants set a team record for 3-point shots made with 142. McCants surpassed the mark set by Isaiah Rider in 1994–95.

ABOVE: Wes Unseld   **RIGHT**: Randy Foye

THE RIGHT STUFF

Randy Foye's heart is on the right side of his body. The point guard has a rare condition called situs inversus. All of his major organs are reversed. Situs inversus occurs in one out of every 10,000 people.

D-UP!

In their first season, the Timberwolves allowed only 99.4 points per game. Only one other team in the NBA had a better defense that year.

REAR IN GEAR

The team's 2008–09 uniform is the first in the NBA with writing across the back of the shorts. The home shorts say "Minnesota," and the road shorts say "Wolves."

DOME SWEET DOME

In 1990, 49,551 fans watched the Timberwolves play the Denver Nuggets in Minnesota's Metrodome. It was the third-largest crowd in NBA history.

Talking Hoops

"I think big. That's what my mother taught me. If you think small and accomplish it, what does it mean? Who cares? To me, the sky's the limit—and I'm going to try to get there."

—Kevin Garnett, on setting goals and achieving them

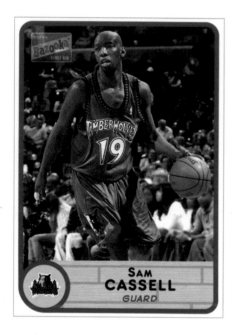

"Sometimes you're going to have to play with pain. You know, this is one of those things where you lead by example. It's an opportunity to show the organization and your teammates your character."

—Latrell Sprewell, on overcoming injuries and staying in the lineup

"I'm a student of the game."

—Sam Cassell, on how he became an NBA star

"Everything for Christian has to do with winning. That's why he's the type of player he is, because of his competitiveness."

—Flip Saunders, on Christian Laettner's reputation as a rough player

"There's some stuff you can't teach. You can't teach toughness. You can't teach being a winner."

—Kevin Love, on what it takes to succeed in the NBA

"I could play ball all day. That's all I want to do."

—Stephon Marbury, on his love of basketball

"I don't necessarily think this is 'my' team, but I'm the one who has to set the example."

—Al Jefferson, on the responsibility of being a young leader

LEFT: Sam Cassell
RIGHT: Kevin Love

For the Record

The great Timberwolves teams and players have left their marks on the record books. These are the "best of the best" …

TIMBERWOLVES AWARD WINNERS

WINNER	AWARD	SEASON
Isaiah Rider	Slam Dunk Champion	1993–94
Kevin Garnett	All-Star Game MVP	2002–03
Kevin Garnett	NBA Most Valuable Player	2003–04

TIMBERWOLVES ACHIEVEMENTS

ACHIEVEMENT	SEASON
Midwest Division Champions	2003–04

LEFT: Isaiah Rider flies toward the rim during the 1994 Slam Dunk Contest.
RIGHT: Kevin Garnett shows his 2004 MVP trophy to the Minnesota fans.

Pinpoints

The history of a basketball team is made up of many smaller stories. These stories take place all over the map—not just in the city a team calls "home." Match the push-pins on these maps to the Team Facts and you will begin to see the story of the Timberwolves unfold!

TEAM FACTS

1   Minneapolis, Minnesota—*The Timberwolves have played here since 1989–90.*

2   Indianapolis, Indiana—*Randy Wittman was born here.*

3   Wooster, Ohio—*Bill Musselman was born here.*

4   Altoona, Pennsylvania—*Doug West was born here.*

5   Angola, New York—*Christian Laettner was born here.*

6   Teaneck, New Jersey—*Tony Campbell was born here.*

7   Baltimore, Maryland—*Sam Cassell was born here.*

8   Mauldin, South Carolina—*Kevin Garnett was born here.*

9   Columbus, Georgia—*Sam Mitchell was born here.*

10   Oakland, California—*Isaiah Rider was born here.*

11   Portland, Oregon—*Terrell Brandon was born here.*

12   Madrid, Spain—*Wally Szczerbiak was born here.*

KEVIN GARNETT
TIMBERWOLVES' **FORWARD**

Kevin Garnett

43

Play Ball

Basketball is a sport played by two teams of five players. NBA games have four 12-minute quarters—48 minutes in all—and the team that scores the most points when time has run out is the winner. Most baskets count for two points. Players who make shots from beyond the three-point line receive an extra point. Baskets made from the free-throw line count for one point. Free throws are penalty shots awarded to a team, usually after an opponent has committed a foul. A foul is called when one player makes hard contact with another.

Players can move around all they want, but the player with the ball cannot. He must bounce the ball with one hand or the other (but never both) in order to go from one part of the court to another. As long as he keeps "dribbling," he can keep moving.

In the NBA, teams must attempt a shot every 24 seconds, so there is little time to waste. The job of the defense is to make it as difficult as possible to take a good shot—and to grab the ball if the other team shoots and misses.

This may sound simple, but anyone who has played the game knows that basketball can be very complicated. Every player on the court has a job to do. Different players have different strengths and weaknesses. The coach must mix these players in just the right way, and teach them to work together as one.

The more you play and watch basketball, the more "little things" you are likely to notice. The next time you are at a game, look for these plays:

ALLEY-OOP—A play where the passer throws the ball just to the side of the rim—so a teammate can catch it and dunk in one motion.

BACK-DOOR PLAY—A play where the passer waits for his teammate to fake the defender away from the basket—then throws him the ball when he cuts back toward the basket.

KICK-OUT—A play where the ball-handler waits for the defense to surround him—then quickly passes to a teammate who is open for an outside shot. The ball is not really kicked in this play; the term comes from the action of pinball machines.

NO-LOOK PASS—A play where the passer fools a defender (with his eyes) into covering one teammate—then suddenly passes to another without looking.

PICK-AND-ROLL—A play where one teammate blocks or "picks off" another's defender with his body—then cuts to the basket for a pass in the confusion.

Glossary

BASKETBALL WORDS TO KNOW

3-POINTER—A shot attempted from behind the 3-point line.

ALL-NBA—An honor given at the end of the season to the NBA's best players at each position.

ALL-ROOKIE—An honor given at the end of the season to the NBA's best first-year players at each position.

ALL-STAR GAME—The annual game in which the best players from the East and the West play against each other. The game does not count in the standings.

AMERICAN BASKETBALL ASSOCIATION (ABA)—The basketball league that played for nine seasons starting in 1967. Prior to the 1976–77 season, four ABA teams joined the NBA, and the rest went out of business.

ASSISTS—Passes that lead to successful shots.

BASELINE—The line that runs behind the basket, from one corner of the court to the other.

BASKETBALL HALL OF FAME—The museum in Springfield, Massachusetts where basketball's greatest players are honored. A player voted into the Hall of Fame is sometimes called a "Hall of Famer."

DRAFT PICKS—College players selected or "drafted" by NBA teams each summer.

MIDWEST DIVISION—A division for teams that play in the central part of the country.

MOST VALUABLE PLAYER (MVP)—The award given each year to the league's best player; also given to the best player in the league finals and All-Star Game.

NATIONAL BASKETBALL ASSOCIATION (NBA)—The professional league that has been operating since 1946–47.

NBA FINALS—The playoff series that decides the champion of the league.

OVERTIME—The extra period played when a game is tied after 48 minutes.

PLAYMAKER—Someone who helps his teammates score by passing the ball.

PLAYOFFS—The games played after the season to determine the league champion.

POSTSEASON—Another term for playoffs.

PROFESSIONAL—A player or team that plays a sport for money. College players are not paid, so they are considered "amateurs."

ROLE PLAYERS—People who are asked to do specific things when they are in a game.

ROOKIE—A player in his first season.

STANDINGS—A daily list of teams, starting with the team with the best record and ending with the team with the worst record.

WESTERN CONFERENCE FINALS—The playoff series that determines which team from the West will play the best team in the East for the NBA Championship.

WOMEN'S NATIONAL BASKETBALL ASSOCIATION (WNBA)—The professional league for women that started in 1996.

OTHER WORDS TO KNOW

AGGRESSIVE—Acting boldly or powerfully.

COMEBACK—The process of catching up from behind, or making up a large deficit.

CONTENDER—A team or person who competes for a championship.

ENTHUSIASM—Strong excitement.

ESPY AWARD—An honor given by the sports network ESPN.

EXPERIENCED—Knowledgeable and skilled in a job.

LOGO—A symbol or design that represents a company or team.

MASCOT—An animal or person believed to bring a group good luck.

MODERNIZED—Brought up to date.

PATIENT—Able to wait calmly.

SATIN—A smooth, shiny fabric.

SETBACKS—Events that slow down or stop a plan.

SYNTHETIC—Made in a laboratory, not in nature.

UNIQUE—Special or one of a kind.

UNVEILED—Made public.

Places to Go

ON THE ROAD

MINNESOTA TIMBERWOLVES
600 First Avenue North
Minneapolis, Minnesota 55403

NAISMITH MEMORIAL BASKETBALL HALL OF FAME
1000 West Columbus Avenue
Springfield, Massachusetts 01105
(877) 4HOOPLA

ON THE WEB

THE NATIONAL BASKETBALL ASSOCIATION   www.nba.com
  • *Learn more about the league's teams, players, and history*

THE MINNESOTA TIMBERWOLVES   www.nba.com/timberwolves
  • *Learn more about the Timberwolves*

THE BASKETBALL HALL OF FAME   www.hoophall.com
  • *Learn more about history's greatest players*

ON THE BOOKSHELF

To learn more about the sport of basketball, look for these books at your library or bookstore:

  • Hareas, John. *Basketball.* New York, New York: DK, 2005.

  • Hughes, Morgan. *Basketball.* Vero Beach, Florida: Rourke Publishing, 2005.

  • Thomas, Keltie. *How Basketball Works.* Berkeley, California: Maple Tree Press, distributed through Publishers Group West, 2005.

Index

PAGE NUMBERS IN **BOLD** REFER TO ILLUSTRATIONS.

The Team

MARK STEWART has written more than 20 books on basketball, and over 100 sports books for kids. He grew up in New York City during the 1960s rooting for the Knicks and Nets, and now takes his two daughters, Mariah and Rachel, to watch them play. Mark comes from a family of writers. His grandfather was Sunday Editor of *The New York Times* and his mother was Articles Editor of *The Ladies Home Journal* and *McCall's*. Mark has profiled hundreds of athletes over the last 20 years. He has also written several books about his native New York, and New Jersey, his home today. Mark is a graduate of Duke University, with a degree in history. He lives with his daughters and wife, Sarah, overlooking Sandy Hook, New Jersey.

MATT ZEYSING is the resident historian at the Basketball Hall of Fame in Springfield, Massachusetts. His research interests include the origins of the game of basketball, the development of professional basketball in the first half of the twentieth century, and the culture and meaning of basketball in American society.